P9-CSE-432

The Rules of a Big Boss

A book of self-love

By

Haelee P. Moone

The Rules of a Big Boss LLC
Knightdale, NC 27545

This book is dedicated to:

Cameron Penix (my little Godsister)

I will not promise you that the road will be easy as you progress through adolescence, young adulthood, and finally adulthood. What I can promise you is that it will be fun and that I will do my best to be there for you each step of the way. My hope is that this book will serve as a roadmap to make things somewhat easier for you as you grow older. I hope that you find it helpful. And who knows, maybe we can write one together when you grow older. Good luck and Godspeed.

Table of Contents

TABLE OF CONTENTS IV

INTRODUCTION 1

PART I: ALL ABOUT ACCEPTANCE SIS 2

RULE NUMBER ONE: FINDING YOURSELF 3
Haters 9
Chapter Summary/Key Takeaways 11
Empower You Exercise One 12
RULE NUMBER TWO: STAYING TRUE TO YOU 17
Changing for A Boy/Girl 21
Choosing Your Path 22
Chapter Summary/Key Takeaways 24
Empower You Exercise Two 25

PART TWO: THIS IS ALL ABOUT YOUR LIFE SIS 31

RULE NUMBER THREE: SHOW ME SOME RESPECT! 32

Respect Yourself 32
Chapter Summary/Key Takeaways 35
Empower You Exercise Three 36
RULE NUMBER FOUR: CONFIDENCE 41
Dear Women of Color 44
LGBTQIA + Community 46
Chapter Summary/Key Takeaways 48
Empower You Exercise Four 49
RULE NUMBER FIVE: IT DOES NOT DEFINE YOU 54

Do Not Allow Yourself to Be Manipulated 58
Take Time for Yourself 59
Chapter Summary/Key Takeaways 60
Empower You Exercise Five 61

EPILOGUE/CONCLUSION 66

WORKS CITED 67

ACKNOWLEDGMENTS 69

CONTACT THE AUTHOR 71

v

Introduction

A lot of people struggle with who they are. This is often rooted in societal standards of what is considered beautiful, acceptable behavior, vogue, cool, etc. These struggles are particularly prevalent in adolescents and young adults. Attempting to fit in can cause you to lose sight of who and what you truly are. I can say this as a matter of fact because it happened and happens to me.

It takes courage to step out of your shell and simply be you. Being you is a freedom and acceptance that you are not and will not be like anyone else. It is a difficult process. You absolutely will not get there overnight. Please know that there are no shortcuts and that you cannot rush it. I say this because you will pick up critical developmental steps along the way. You will miss those steps if you rush through everything.

While I can help inspire you, I cannot help in making you more confident in yourself. That is a journey that you will have to travel alone. The good news is that I will do what I can to support you along the way. It is my hope that this book helps serve that purpose in a sense. As a special note, the things contained within are what help me daily. In writing this book I am not only helping you but helping myself too. Good luck, Godspeed, I hope you enjoy it, and thank you for purchasing it!

PART I: All About Acceptance Sis

You will learn how to accept yourself in this part. This is important to your wellbeing. Please know that you are special. Do not let anyone ever tell you that you are not. The truth is some people will tell you otherwise. It might result in you feeling a little bit lower about yourself over time. Please come to me if you ever have doubts so that I can remind and assure you of how special you are, as this is important for your growth. Do not worry about a thing Sis. I got you. We are going to get you set. Let's get it poppin' and have fun y'all.

Rule Number One: Finding Yourself

Like and find what is comfortable for you. Do not stick with things that feel unnatural or uncomfortable. I for one have altered my style and vibe many times over the years. The beauty of hindsight is that it gives you 20/20 vision. I say this because I looked crazy over the years. My eyebrows are very thin, so I decided to try something new when I was in the fourth grade. I decided within myself to put some eyeshadow on to darken them. Chile listen I thought that I was poppin', that is until I got to school. People were staring at me throughout the morning. It necessitated in me taking a trip to the bathroom so that I could look at myself in the mirror with a critical eye. I realized then that I looked like a complete fool. I took it all in stride though because it was risky. It afforded me a chance to laugh at myself while proceeding on the journey towards self-discovery. What I am saying here is that I am glad that I did it because I learned that it was not me.

Sometimes the only way to learn who you are is to learn who you are not. Experiment on yourself to find out what you like. Putting outfits together in your room and just going with the flow helps. You will look God-awful at times and that is okay. You will look and feel like a whole baddie at other times (e.g. Rihanna). Please do not allow yourself to get down if your look does not come out the way that you hoped. Just try again and keep going until it feels right. Please also know that you are uniquely beautiful. The outfit does not make you; you make it. So, feel free to experiment and rock with it.

I love music of various genres. Some of those include Pop, R&B, Gospel, and Hip Hop. Listening to different genres and artists helps with self-discovery as it allows you to step outside of your comfort zone. That is important because most artists are not married to one genre throughout their career. My Dad was and has been a huge influence in that regard. We listened to a lot of Michael Jackson, Mary J Blige, Fred Hammond, and JAY-Z on many of our car rides. This has led me to discover that I love old school R&B. My Dad will laugh and rub it in if he ever finds out. He will specifically say that I am a Daddy's Girl while singing this God-awful song that he made up for me. It goes, "I'm a Daddy's Girl, I live in his world. I like to spin and twirl because I'm his little pearl." I cannot stand when he sings it so please let this be our little secret [Shh].

As far as beauty goes, more specifically makeup, you do not have to purchase or wear a great deal of it. Please note that I am by no means saying that you should not wear it. It is not my ministry to tell you that. I simply want you to recall that you are uniquely beautiful in your own rite. As a matter of fact, you should start off each day by telling yourself that. Moving along, I personally discovered that I prefer more of a natural look for myself. I reached this conclusion through experimentation and self-discovery. I watched my Grandma, Mom, and Aunts apply makeup when I was younger. I asked if I could try some on for curiosity sakes. They were happy to let me experiment [just a little bit]. I mean us ladies must be fabulous, fly, and fancy. That is an absolute must (LOL). While I previously prefaced that I prefer a natural look, I do have some makeup of my own. I experiment with it from time to time just to switch up my vibe and move along that journey towards self-discovery. I strongly suggest that you watch makeup tutorials, look at pictures online, and most of all check out your mom or favorite aunt.

    I have always felt like my Dad did not particularly approve of my style choices. That has contributed towards some insecurities within me. For example, he loves to take me shopping at Justice and Old Navy. While I like the latter's bottoms, I do not like their tops by any means. Their tops make me feel like a mom or a grandma. What's more, their selection of tops makes me feel off beat because it does not fit my personality or vibe. Now to his defense, he does let me pick out what I want for the most part [within reason] but I still do not like it. I prefer to shop at places such as H&M, Forever 21, Romwe, Shein, Pretty Little Thing, and Fashion Nova. Those stores have cute, high-quality, and empowering clothing. My Dad shows a complete lack of interest when I attempt to show him things from those retailers. What's more he typically says, "No" when I ask him can we go look around in them with exceptions being H&M and Forever 21. His logic is that he does not want me to rush to grow up and I understand that, but he must realize that I am and will grow up. He must let me break out of my shell somewhat. Your parents will have to do the same. I cannot really argue with my

Dad about store selection because he is spending his coins and I am still a teenager. He does give me a weekly allowance in exchange for chores. Because of this, I have made a conscious decision that I will save up my coins. In doing so, my plan is that I will start buying my own things little by little and piece by piece.

Now let's talk about copying. Please do not mimic other people's style or vibe. I say this because you will lose yourself in doing so. As a case in point, I tried to mimic Aaliyah's style with my clothing and hair. I did this because I did not know how to style myself. I needed inspiration in that regard. I looked cute on the surface, but I did not feel good about it once I put it on. The reason being is that it simply was not me. What I am saying in that sense is while some things may look cute, they do not necessarily suit you. You should simply use other people's style as a baseline to create your own style and vibe. Please note, that it is important to be inspired but not copied. If I am being completely honest, finding yourself is somewhat easy. Sticking with it is much harder. The reason being is that societal pressures will always tell you that this is right, and that is wrong. Finding what is right for you is a delicate balance but you will get there through persistence. What I am saying here is that it is going to take time. Please be patient. The final output will be so worth it in the end. You will create a path for others to be inspired in finding yourself. People will feel inspired by witnessing your glow up. Adolescents and young adults are often tempted and do mimic the behaviors and personalities of their favorite celebrities, athletes, etc. The reason being is that we are impressionable. As stated previously you lose yourself in mimicking others so please just do not do it Sis. Please just explore yourself and your surroundings. You will find what you enjoy and who you are in due time having done so. It took me a few years to fully embrace myself in large because I used to want to be just like everyone else particularly the popular girls that were around my age. I realized in time that I was unhappy in doing so because everything felt so unnatural. What I am saying here is that you should always stay true to yourself in large because everyone else is taken. Now here is how you do it:

1. *Music on*

2. *New hair style*

3. *A little makeup or lip gloss*

4. *New outfit that you put together*

5. *Mirror up*

6. *Now strut around your room*

I do these six things at least twice per week. I call them my, "Vibe Sessions." I allow myself to get lost in the aura of the music and clothing but most of all I have fun. They will literally have you feeling like a Bad Mama Jama. Oh gosh, I cannot believe I just said that (LOL). Any-who have fun with it and find yourself. Please also remember that you are uniquely beautiful as I said before.

Haters

You just know that you are looking good after you complete your Vibe Session as referenced in Rule Number One. You are now ready to enter the social outing, the school, or step on the school bus, but you notice something off-putting. You observe that the group of haters (mean girls) are rolling their eyes and undressing you with nasty looks. You even overheard a few of them demean you in some way. Well that is totally okay Sis and I am here to tell you why. Haters are motivators. They are evidence that you are doing something right. And so, what if they do not like your outfit or your hairstyle. I mean they are not the ones that are wearing it right?

Mean girls may not let you sit with them on the bus or in the cafeteria. They may not even want to be seen talking with you in the hallway. They may not consider you as trendy or lit, but the truth is that they have stale viewpoints of what is trendy. While I hate people like that, I do not let them bother me. I simply laugh, flip my hair, and walk away. My attitude in doing so is simply, "Honey you wish that you could be as poppin' as me." What I am saying here is if you like your personal style, I love it. Do not allow them or anyone for that matter to make you feel insecure or self-conscious in any way, shape, or form. Please feel free to be unapologetically you. You know who you are and what you enjoy so do you boo as you own your style and vibe.

You are inclined to encounter frenemies on your journey towards self-discovery. A frenemy is someone who presents themselves as a friend, but they are secretly your enemy. To coin an old phrase, they are also known as wolves in sheep's clothing. These individuals will often try and manipulate you in ways that suit them. Those ways are often times harmful and damaging to you. They do this because they are unhappy with something within themselves and misery loves company. You do not need these types of people in your life at all Sis. You need to cut them off as soon as you notice that they are moving funny. Doing so is empowering in that it allows you to maintain your shine before they ever try and bring you down. You have the power to control your own vibe. You can do this by making the decisions that are best for you in determining who you allow to remain in your circle and who you remove from it. Make the decisions that are best for your shine.

Moving along, Mary J Blige has a song called, "I Feel Good." The chorus to the song reads/sings, "I feel good, like the moon is shinin' just for me. Tonight, I'm fly as I can be. Don't you try to bring me down though. It's not like you could. I feel too damn good." This song can be found on her Stronger with Each Tear Album. You can literally stream it from any music platform to include Apple, YouTube, or Amazon. I mention this because the song is all about self-esteem and empowerment. You need to bake the lyrics of the song into your memory. No one will ever be able to steal your shine once you not only know the lyrics but believe them so get to work on memorizing them Sis.

Chapter Summary/Key Takeaways

1. *Spend time with yourself*

2. *Learn yourself*

3. *Do what works best for you*

4. *Have fun learning you*

Empower You Exercise One

Please use this area to describe what you have learned about yourself. Please also share how and why it is important.

Please use this space to share how you feel after reading this chapter.

Please use this area to describe why you believe "Vibe Sections" are important. Please also share when you intend to have your first session.

Please use this area to describe your personal style.

In the next chapter, you will learn...

How to stay true to yourself. This will be difficult but nothing in life worth having comes easy. You must work hard for those things. Remember that you are going to have off days here and there. I can give you tips on how to go about making your worst days brighter, but I cannot help you see things as perfect. I say this because perfection is impossible so you must not get caught up in expecting it. My hope is that this chapter helps empower you in seeing the brighter side of things.

Rule Number Two: Staying True to You

Rule number two might be the most difficult of all to follow. The reason being is that we all have an underlying desire to want to fit in. Societal pressures are ever more pressing for adolescents, young ladies, and even grown women. We are told how we should wear our hair, dress, what shoes we should wear, etc. As far as clothing goes, crop tops, booty shorts, Crocs, and Vans are trendy with respect to my generation. While I like some of these items, I do not necessarily abide by those style trends. The reason being is that everything is not for everyone. Many of those things do not even fit my figure. Not only that but they do not mix with my morals, personal vibe, and style.

Moving along we are told by society that we are too big or too small and too light or too dark in other cases. These things are often said to us when we are really young, so the seeds are already planted deep within us. That results in us not embracing the reflection that we see in the mirror. We end up becoming our worst critic as a result of this. We end up spending a lot of money on fad diets, cosmetic surgeries, etc. to look like someone or something else. While I am still a young lady, I know full well what women do to fit into those dresses that they have been saving for a special occasion or better yet that swimsuit that they have been saving for their next vacation. Please just wear what compliments your figure and personality. Those things are what are truly poppin' in my opinion. Now I am by no means saying that you should not go on diets or anything like that. I am simply saying do not lose sight of yourself in the process of it. I am also saying embrace your own unique beauty and style. You are naturally beautiful Sis so rock with it.

Peer pressure is something else that you will have to worry about along the way. Peer pressure is defined as, "influence from members of one's peer and/or social group." Victims are made to feel as if they will no longer fit in if they do not conform to the wants and desires of the group. As an example, yourself and a group of frenemies may go into H&M or some other type of store. Those frenemies may dare you to prove your loyalty by stealing something. You know that it is morally wrong because your parents have taught you better than that. What's more you know that your parents would probably buy it for you if you only asked. You feel pressured to take the dare because you are so desperate to fit in or rather continuing to fit in, so you go ahead and steal the item. You then find yourself accosted by security and your frenemies nowhere to be found. You then have to call your parents, explain what happened, and hope that they are able and willing to get you out of the mess that you have dug for yourself. Your parents may be able to in some cases but not all. It can and will affect your future ability to go to college and work at certain jobs if your parents are unable to clear your criminal record. You must be strong enough to simply say, "No."

I mistakenly spent a good portion of my life trying to fit in and being a people pleaser. This led to my trying to be a mean girl so that I could fit in. That only led to my ending up in the principal's office and on punishment. I also tried being the nice girl. That resulted in me getting my feelings hurt because I was giving out more of myself than I was receiving in return. Nothing that I attempted brought me the attention that I desired. I learned through those events that a lot of people will not be pleased no matter what you do. That had a negative effect on my self-esteem in that I did not believe that I could do anything right. That led to feelings of unhappiness and depression within me. I had to learn that I do not and did not need a huge group of friends or a social group at the end of the day. You will have to learn these lessons as well Sis. You literally have everything that you need within yourself and God. You were placed on this Earth to please Him and Him alone. You should simply live your life and do so unapologetically. He loves you and so do I. You should love yourself too. You will become your own best friend in time. I say these things as a matter of fact because I am my own best friend. The reason being is because no one knows or understands me better than my own self. My Dad does not fall too far behind but please do not tell him that I said so because he will start with that God-awful song that I referenced earlier. I promise that you are and have more than enough Sis. Please revisit your "Vibe Session," add your own flare to whatever, embrace it, and rock with it. I promise you will appreciate it so much more. The reason being is that it is unapologetically you.

Changing for A Boy/Girl

No ma'am, please do not ever do this. That person will not like or love you for who and what you are. They will prefer your representative over you. That places you in a position of having to put on a constant front as opposed to simply being you. Now let's unpack that for a moment. Do you want to go through life pretending to be something or someone that you are not? While that question is rhetorical, the answer to it should be a resounding, "No."

To borrow a quote from my Grandma, "I can do bad by my damn self." There is nothing wrong with spending time with yourself. I know it sounds cliché, but all good things come to those who wait. There literally is someone out there for everyone. On that note, you must be patient in knowing what is for you and you alone. Outkast has a song called, "In Due Time." The chorus of the song reads/sings, "Just keep your faith in me. Don't act impatiently. You'll get where you need to be in due time. Even when things go slow. Hold on and don't let go. I'll give you what I owe in due time." This song can be found on the Soul Food Soundtrack. It is like the Mary J Blige song referenced earlier in that it can be streamed from multiple music platforms. You should take time to bake the lyrics into memory as they are well served in the development of patience.

You should spend your season of singlehood pampering and bettering yourself physically, mentally, and spiritually. This can be done by giving yourself

21

manicures/pedicures, trying new makeup blends, vision boarding, journaling, exercising, or binge watching a tv show. These things will contribute towards your personal happiness. You will be better not only to yourself but others as well once you get to that point. That will equip you to receive the love that you need, desire, and deserve. Trust me Sis, things always work out in the end for those that are faithful and true to themselves so please do these few things.

Choosing Your Path

An old saying reads, "Opinions are like assholes, everybody's got one and everyone thinks everyone else's stinks." What this means is that you cannot please everyone. You should discover what pleases you, embrace it, and walk in it. To do otherwise will lead towards discontent given enough time. To be specific my Dad went to school for Engineering and IT. My Grandparents steered him in that direction because he had a natural gift for STEM. He also told me that it was unlikely that he would have been able to make the same money in Human Services. I mention Human Services because it speaks more towards his heart. My Dad advised me that he wishes that he would have went to school for Psychology or Education because he genuinely enjoys helping people.

While I do not know the exact specifics, my Dad informed me that he reached a point of burnout with IT. The reason being is that he was never happy doing IT based work. He was simply trying to please others, chase money, and walk in one of his gifts. My Dad genuinely cares about others so I believe that he would have succeeded as a Psychologist or Psychiatrist. Given those lessons, he has advised me that chasing after money is like a dog chasing its tail. A dog rarely catches it. Money does not bring happiness. Happiness is found in doing and appreciating those things that you love. Those that are happy have the true riches of life. You should do what you want to do because it is your life and no one else's. I personally want to go to Law School. My Dad tells me that I will do great at it because I love to debate people, but time will tell.

Bad Vibes

Bad vibes are all around us. They literally attach to people. With that in mind, you must be careful who you hang around and allow within your inner circle. The reason being is that other people's bad vibes can rub off on you given enough time. You will find yourself changing in due time. As a case in point, I used to be friends with someone who made it their mission to retaliate against anyone that she perceived to have disrespected her in any way. I was the exact opposite however in that I would let things roll off my back and just walk away. Her toxic need for revenge rubbed off on me in time in that I soon found myself feeling the need to retaliate against every perceived slight. That resulted in me ending up in the principal's office and on punishment yet again. She and I are no longer friends in large because I realized that I was becoming someone that I did not like through my association with her. What's more, I realized in time that I was more of a friend to her than she ever was or could be to me. On that note, you must know that people with bad vibes are like snakes. They will lure you in with a sultry dance only to bite you when you let your guard down.

Chapter Summary/Key Takeaways

1. *Choose your friends wisely*

2. *Stay true to yourself*

3. *Avoid bad vibes*

Empower You Exercise Two

Please use this section to describe what you learned in this chapter.

Please use this section to describe if it is right to live for someone else. If not, why not?

Please use this section to describe how it feels to stay true to yourself.

Please use this section to map out your path.

Please use this section to describe if it is ever appropriate to change for another person. If not, why not?

In the next chapter, you will learn...

How to deal with people in a way that shows respect towards yourself.

Part Two: This Is All About Your Life Sis

The information contained within this chapter has no age limit. It is literally for everyone young and old in that sense. You will learn about respect within. This is of utmost importance because it is one of the keys towards living your best life. I am not going to lie and tell you that I am some type of expert because I am not. I am literally learning many of these things at the time of this writing. The beauty of this is that we can go on this journey of exploration and learning together.

Rule Number Three: Show Me Some Respect!

You are deserving of the utmost respect and love. Please know that respect is not given. It must be earned. You earn it by readily giving it to others. What I am saying in that sense is please do not tear others down to gain clout. You will lose sight of yourself in doing so. That will lead towards a lack of respect for your own-self and from others. Respect towards self and others exudes confidence and beauty. And I Stan that.

Respect Yourself

Self-respect is critical in your journey toward self-discovery. You absolutely must treat yourself with confidence and kindness. You do this by speaking affirmations into the atmosphere. Speak positive things with respect to yourself. Examples of this are, "I surround myself with positive people," "I have a positive body image," "I am enough," "I have an overflow," "I am worth the fight," etc. These things tie into what is known as the Law of Attraction. The Law of Attraction uses positive thought affirmation to manifest positive things in your life. You will receive whatever you focus your mind and energy on. You will literally receive all good things if you focus your energy on positive thoughts. Given that

32

sentiment, please radiate that good loving energy and watch how it pays off.

Moving along, people do not respect individuals who do not respect themselves. Given that sentiment you must stand up to individuals who attempt to disrespect you. You should not by any means seek to avenge yourself whenever someone slights you. It simply means that you let them know that you will not tolerate any nonsense or disrespect from them, and you walk away. You walk away because everyone is not worthy of your time or energy. An old saying goes, "Arguing with fools proves that there are two." Given those sentiments, going back and forth with them is of minimal value to you.

My former best friend had a habit of talking down to me. She would literally point out each one of my flaws and highlight my mistakes. It had a negative effect on my self-esteem over time. I began to feel like less than because of it all. I resultantly had a talk with my Dad, but I did not do it right away. He reminded me who and what am. I am a Lioness. A Lioness protects her pack when the King is away. On that note, he advised me that I needed to stand up for myself and fight back. I responded by telling her about herself, letting her know that I would not take any more of her mess, and that I was ending our friendship. She humbled herself immediately thereafter in asking for forgiveness and changing her attitude. While I accepted her apology, I refused to be friends again. I felt liberated and empowered because I had regained a part of myself that I allowed her to

33

take away. What I am saying here is rise up and show the strength of the Lioness that you are when you are pressured. There will be times when you cannot walk away, however. You must be prepared to stand up and fight in those instances where it is necessary as a result. What I am saying in that regard is walk away where you can but do not be a doormat.

Queens fix and adjust one another's crowns so you should respect others. That means that we lift each other up as opposed to tearing one another down. Those that do otherwise reek of insecurity and disrespect. I wish that I could say that my hands are clean in that regard, but they are not. As mentioned previously I am guilty of once being a mean girl. I am by no means proud of that and I am truly remorseful for my actions. I have grown to know better and do better. The key to getting to that point in life was fully accepting myself for who and what I am. I now receive respect from others because I give it. Remember what I said about the Law of Attraction?

Chapter Summary/Key Takeaways

1. *Respect yourself*

2. *Respect others*

Empower You Exercise Three

Please use this section to describe ways that you can go about showing respect for yourself.

Please use this area to describe ways that you can be respectful towards others.

Please use this section to describe how it makes you feel when you are being respected by others.

Please use this section to describe any difficulties that you may have in showing respect to others.

In the next chapter, you will learn...

Confidence is defined as, "a feeling or consciousness of one's powers or of reliance on one's circumstances." Confidence is critical in your journey towards self-discovery and being a big boss. This section will address that.

Rule Number Four: Confidence

We have all been stuck in the house over the past several months due to COVID-19. This has prevented many of us from getting our hair, nails, and feet done. But, so what. Pampering is minor at the end of the day. It does not compare to our health, safety, and physical well-being. I know that is much easier said than done in large because we are used to looking a certain way. Notwithstanding we must train our mind and spirit to see outside the box. We must remember that we are baddies with or without our glow-up. Recognizing this requires some creative ingenuity of sorts. We absolutely must act like our hair and nails are done. We ought to dress up and go somewhere, anywhere. It does not matter if it is to the kitchen, mailbox, or to walk our fur babies, we absolutely must get outside of our respective bedrooms and houses. In stepping outside we must have the attitude in knowing that we are, "That Chick." And do you know why? It is because we are fabulous, we are queens/princesses, and we are important. Statements of affirmation help improve our overall mindset, environment, and confidence. Given that sentiment we must train our mind to not only speak but believe those things. Confidence is attractive so embrace it and rock with it Sis.

Social media influencers are seen as being authoritative figures in the areas of fashion, beauty, products, and services. They influence the market and trends through their sizeable social media footprint.

They present themselves as the standard for beauty and living the best lives. We all want to live life more abundantly. As such we make the mistake of comparing ourselves to them and their lives. We find ourselves wishing that we had what they have or could go where they have been. Insecurities begin to creep in at that point. This is absent of gender in that both [young] men and [young] women are guilty of doing it. But let me tell you something honey, those things that you see on social media are not real. People are literally living their best lives on a surgeons table and through filters. They underwent surgery to get that perfect body, they use filters to remove their blemishes, they use Photoshop to transpose themselves into luxurious places, etc. But what happens when the camera goes off? Are those individuals truly living their best lives? Many of them are unhappy within themselves. Quite a few come from abusive homes, suffer from personality disorders, have low self-esteem, etc. The casual observer may not know this because social media influencers have mastered the art of finessing. Finessing is the act of playing someone. I for one know better in that not all of them are living their best lives. I know this because I have receipts. I will not pull them out however because queens adjust each other's crowns as I said before. I guess what I am saying here is that we do not truly know what goes on in an individual's personal life or what type of demons that they are battling. They may be battling something that we are not equipped to handle so we should not want to walk in their shoes. We should not aspire to be like them or have their lives for those reasons alone. We should appreciate the life that God has given us because it is uniquely made for us.

The most important aspect of confidence is self-love. I like you, struggle with this at times. The reason being is that I suffer from acne. I mean we all have individual insecurities, right? At any rate, I use a variety of products by Clinique to combat and minimize it, but the imperfections remain. I literally see them whenever I look in the mirror. I feel the imperfections whenever I rub my hands across my face. That aside, it is beyond my control for the most part, so I do not give it much energy. Giving energy to our flaws dulls our shine. I am not about that life Sis, so I focus on what is positive about myself by speaking affirmations. As a specific example, I tell myself, "I am sun-kissed," "My skin absolutely glows in the sunlight," "I am dripping melanin baby." Everyone cannot say the same so that gives me a reason to be thankful. You may not be able to say those exact same things about yourself and that is perfectly okay Sis. It is okay because they are my individual affirmation not yours. You should spend some time finding what speaks life into you as a specific individual. You will be able to see yourself and the beauty that you exude when you are able to speak that life into yourself. We may not have the ideal body or skin, but we are uniquely and wonderfully made as God intended for us to be. The very things that make us different are what make us beautiful.

I have seen some outfits that looked God-awful on the rack, but they looked great when I or someone put them on. And do you know why? It is because you make the outfit as I said before. Confidence has transformative power. Given that sentiment you should not worry that you do not have the trendiest clothes and accessories. You should always feel comfortable in your own skin and take pride in who you are. You can achieve this by always revisiting your "Vibe Sessions." You should exit them in knowing that you are "That Chick." Re-enter or remain within your session if you are not quite feeling it yet. Confidence looks great on you. You should wear it every day.

Dear Women of Color

Malcolm X said, "The most disrespected person in America is the black woman. The most unprotected person in America is the black woman. The most neglected person in America is the black woman." He was speaking towards the degree of discrimination and lack of protections that women experienced back then. What's sad is those statements remain true today. The generations of disrespect have led to the development of self-hate in many cases. While I am young, I know this to be accurate because it was formerly true for me. Not only that but my Grandma, my Mom, and my Aunts have shared with me that they once felt the same way. As for me, I hated my sun-kissed skin and kinky brown hair. I wanted to be anything other than what God created me to be. I very much wanted to be like Rapunzel from Tangled. Rapunzel had long flowing blond hair, milky smooth skin, blue eyes, and a small waist. She was the epitome of what was considered beautiful in that regard (European Standard). Disney has become more culturally diverse over time with the development of Princess Tiana, Moana, and Pocahontas as characters, but they are outliers in the grand scheme of things. I say this in part because it is not often that you see women of color on the cover of magazines and other print materials unless it is specifically catered towards African Americans. What's more those women are rarely built like me or the women that I see in everyday life. I did not begin to embrace the beauty of the skin that I was in until my Dad brought me a [children's] book called, "It's All Good: A Book About Self Acceptance & Diversity" by Gina Humber. The book helps young readers improve their personal image through acceptance of themselves.

Self-hate is not exclusive to women of color by any means. Men of color exude self-hate too. Some of them date outside their race because they hate the skin that they are in. They resultantly date Caucasian women because they believe that it elevates them. They tend to tear down black women in the process by saying things such as, "We are too aggressive," "We are too independent," "We are too opinionated," and "We are too angry." They even state that they would never have children with us because they would turn out ugly. To that end, they imply that they would rather have children with

45

Caucasian women because they believe that fair skinned, curly hair children are beautiful. It is quite sad because they were born of women of color. Their thoughts and sentiments imply that they not only hate themselves but their own mothers too.

The seeds of self-hate have taken further root by way of Donald Trump. Mr. Trump has told African Americans and other minorities to go back where we came from as if we were not citizens of the United States. Not only that but he has inappropriately miscast Hispanics as drug dealers and rapist, Native Americans as barbarians and savages, and Asian people as asymptomatic carriers of COVID-19. The cumulative effect of these things over time will have a negative effect on our self-esteem if we allow it. That is part of his plan. He wants to beat us down to make us feel less than. He literally feels elevated as he lessens and cheapens us. We cannot allow that to happen, Sis. You must recognize that you are not only beautiful but marvelous in your own way. You are in fact exactly how God designed you to be.

LGBTQIA + Community

While I am a heterosexual Christian, I believe that everyone is entitled to love whomever they want. You should be free to do this irrespective of sexuality, ethnicity, skin color, or religion. I know that everyone does not share my views in that respect, so it creates a dilemma for you. That dilemma often causes you to hide who you are from family, friends, co-workers,

46

religious leaders, etc. It might even cause you to hide who you truly are from your own self in some cases. With respect to religion, I know that the Bible says that God created woman for man. I also know that God destroyed Sodom and Gomorrah. A lot of religious leaders like to reference the destruction of Sodom and Gomorrah as evidence of God's disdain for your lifestyle. In doing so they infer that you will be relegated to Hell if you do not turn back from it and choose a heterosexual lifestyle. I do not believe in a God that operates that way. I say that in part because He gave us the gift of autonomy. Jesus literally said that He is the only way to the Father. To be specific His exact words were, "I am the way and the truth and the life. No one comes to the Father except through me." John 3:16 reads, "For God so loved the world that he gave his one and only Son, that whoever believes in him shall not perish but have eternal life." What this means is that whoever believes in Him shall be welcomed into the Kingdom. I nor anyone for that matter has a Heaven or Hell to put you in. You and you alone make that decision about your final resting place. It is all rooted in whether you believe in the Father, Son, and Holy Ghost.

My hope is that the things that I shared above will afford you some comfort in being able to walk in your truth. I know that that is much easier said than done. Everyone is not going to be as accepting as I am and that is okay. You are more than equipped to handle it. Wear your confidence and rock with it. What I am saying in all of this is, "You matter too."

Chapter Summary/Key Takeaways

1. *Self-hate vs Self-love*

2. *You matter too*

Empower You Exercise Four

Please use this section to describe how confidence makes you feel. Please also share why it is important.

Please use this section to share ways that you go about wearing your confidence.

Please use this section to share what takes away from your confidence. Please also use it to write out ways in which you can avoid it being taken away from you.

Please use this section to describe ways in which you can improve your confidence within yourself.

In the next chapter, you will learn...

How to cope with anxiety and depression and rise against it. Anxiety is defined as, "Apprehensive uneasiness or nervousness usually over an impending or anticipated ill." Depression is a medical condition that affects the way that you feel and act. It tends to present itself as being consistently sad.

Rule Number Five: It Does Not Define You

While I am no expert, I know that anxiety and depression can lead to dangerous consequences left untreated. Those consequences can include harming others and/or yourself in extreme cases. I will share a personal story about my bout with anxiety and depression in the text below.

I was close friends with this other girl. We shall call her Anonymous for the context of this writing. Anonymous and I lived a few houses down from one another and we went to the same school. That afforded us plenty of time to establish bonds not only with us but our parents as well. Anonymous and her mother invited me over to her house one day for a play date and party. My Dad had never been the type to let me out of his sight much, but he allowed it given the proximity and the bonds that had been forged. Anonymous and I were having a good time playing in her room, but things took a change for the worse. Anonymous pinned me against a wall and attempted to kiss me. I evaded her attempt by covering my mouth and turning my head away in refusal. I mean my own parents have never kissed me in my mouth to my knowledge, but I digress. Anonymous then attempted to put her hands down my pants so that she could touch my private parts. I again blocked her. I exited her room immediately thereafter and requested to go home. While I was not yet mature enough to unpack all the pieces of what

54

occurred, I could not think of a time when I was happier to see my Dad.

I did not tell my Dad what occurred right away, but I told him that I did not want to be her friend anymore. I cannot speak as to why I did not tell him right away other than I did not understand what occurred nor how to tell him. I did eventually tell him though. My Dad attempted to talk with her mother about it and other matters, but the conversation did not go so well. The adults agreed that the children nor themselves would have any further contact with one another going forward.

Anonymous started bullying me immediately thereafter. She did this by attempting to strangle me, drown me, and spreading rumors about me amongst classmates and mutual friends. My Dad did all that he could in taking me to counseling, fighting with the school system, encouraging me to fight back, and taking the other family to court. But the damage was already done in that I was depressed. I was resultantly afraid to not only go outside and play but also to go to school. I was afraid to go to school in large because the teachers nor principal ever believed me when I told them about what was occurring. They literally thought that I was making everything up because they had only seen Anonymous be a sweet little girl. On that note, they accused me of projecting as if I were the problem as opposed to her. To be blunt about things, they did not take the issues seriously by any means. I cannot figure out for the life of me why that was the case. Was it because my black life did not matter to them? Was it because me too did not matter to them? Whatever the case may have been I knew that it was wrong and that I was afraid. I oft times faked illness so that I would not have to deal with Anonymous. I would quietly sulk and second guess myself as I sat in my room. I would blame myself in doing so as if I were the reason that these things were happening to me. I wondered aloud what I could possibly do to make it all end. I wondered if I and everyone would be better off if I just committed suicide.

My Dad encouraged me and supported me the best way that he knew how through it all. He told me that I had to take a stand for myself and fight back at some point. He literally said to me, "I know that you know how to fight because I taught you. She will leave you alone once you beat her ass. Why won't you fight her back?" I never had an answer for him in response. I would simply cry. My tears held the answer that my mouth could not speak. The answer was, "I'm scared." I suppose my Dad finally realized that that was the case over time because he finally said to me, "I cannot fight every battle for you. I have literally taken on the County Executive, Congress, School Board, Juvenile Services, and the Police in defense of you. Hell, I even called up President Obama. You have to stand up for yourself at some point because I cannot and will not be there to fight every battle for you." He added to that, "Go outside and play. Come in the house and get me if Anonymous puts her hands on you and I will come outside. I will make certain that she does not beat you up or hurt you again." Baby those words were like music to my ears in that I finally put the nice girl away. I beat Anonymous like a drum. She ran in the house crying to her parents when I got finished with her. I am by no means condoning violence but Baby it felt good to reclaim that sense of myself by fighting back.

Moving along, you must treat anxiety and depression like I treated Anonymous. You must fight it the best way that you can. You must tell it that it will not beat you down as you attempt to regain your sense of peace. You must tell it that enough is enough. There is of course no one size fits all solution in fighting depressions nor anxiety. What works for one will not necessarily work for the other. The fun of it all is that you have the power to choose and explore what works best for you. You do this by discovering what specific things lift your spirit and improve your mindset. While this is by no means an all-inclusive list, you can do something as simple as listening to uplifting music, coloring, journaling, practicing yoga, or exercising to name a few. But most of all you should absolutely seek professional help as it is available to you. It is well past time that we get rid of the stigmas surrounding mental health in the African American Community. A healthy mind and spirit look great on you.

Do Not Allow Yourself to Be Manipulated

Manipulation can play a huge role in depression and anxiety. A specific example of this can be found where you attempt to confront someone about how they have made you feel about something or the other. That person in turn responds by saying something to the effect that they did this because you did this or rather, I did that because you did not do this. What I am saying here is that they twist things to make it appear that their actions were a result of a reaction to you as opposed them simply being wrong. People like this will have you second guessing yourself constantly in believing that you are a bad person when it is really them. They do this because they lack accountability for their own behaviors and actions. That is called gas-lighting Sis. Donald Trump is an expert in it. My advice is to remove yourself immediately when you find yourself engaged with someone who is a gas-lighter. You will find yourself crashing and passing out in due time if you allow yourself to be subjected to their deadly fumes for too long. What that means is that you will soon find yourself in a state of anxiety, depression, and second guessing yourself.

Take Time for Yourself

As I said before, you are or rather should be your best friend. Please spend some time discovering and being kinder to yourself. You can do this by pampering yourself or simply vegging out. These things are known as essential self-maintenance. Take care of your mental health Sis and please do not let anyone steal your shine.

Chapter Summary/Key Takeaways

1. *Mental health*

2. *Fighting back*

Empower You Exercise Five

Please use this section to describe what makes you feel depressed or anxious.

Please use this section to describe what relaxes and calms you.

Please use this section to describe how you can go about improving your mental health.

Please use this section to outline how you will go about taking time out for yourself.

Please use this section to describe how you feel after reading this book.

Epilogue/Conclusion

This book was created for educational purposes. The intent behind it was to help give you some tools to boost your self-esteem. Please love yourself, stay true to yourself, find your vibe, and take care. Please also remember that no one else's opinion about your life and choices matter beyond your own.

Works Cited

"Anxiety." Merriam-Webster.com Dictionary,
Merriam-Webster,
    https://www.merriam-
webster.com/dictionary/anxiety. Accessed 24 Jun.
2020.

"A Quote by Doris M. Smith." Goodreads,
Goodreads,
    https://www.goodreads.com/quotes/31379-
arguing-with-a-fool-proves-there-are-two.

"Confidence." Merriam-Webster.com Dictionary,
Merriam-Webster,
    https://www.merriam-
webster.com/dictionary/confidence. Accessed 24
Jun. 2020.

Elkeles, Simone. How to Ruin a Summer Vacation.
Flux, 2006.

Emba, Christine. "Who Cares about Little Black
Girls." The Houston Chronicle, 11 Jan. 2019.

"Peer pressure." Merriam-Webster.com Dictionary,
Merriam-Webster,

https://www.merriam-webster.com/dictionary/peer%20pressure. Accessed 24 Jun. 2020.

The Holy Bible. NIV. Biblica, 2011.

Acknowledgments

I have been through some dark times in my young life. I guess it was all for a purpose however in that they helped me write this book. That lets me know that my pain had a purpose. It lets me know that my life has purpose. On that note, I would like to take a moment to thank and acknowledge the following people in helping me put this entire thing together.

1. God for his grace and mercies that renew daily.

2. My Dad, Dedrick L. Moone for supporting and being there for me no matter the occasion.

3. My Grandma, Wanda R. Moone for her old sayings and makeup.

4. My Mom, Melanie P. Baltimore for teaching me about affirmations.

5. Dr. Vanessa J. Raynor for her suggestions and edits.

6. Myanna and Rachel for being my closest friends outside of myself (LOL).

7. Tanikwa Matthews for purchasing an advance copy and investing in my publishing rights.

8. Oreo, for emotional support.

Words cannot begin to express how grateful I am to each one of you outlined above. I am excited to find out what the next chapter foretells for each one of us going forward. I

Contact the Author

You can connect the author via either social media or the web. Details are provided below. She hopes to hear from you.

	https://www.thebookofselflove.com
	@thebookofselflove2020
	@thebookofselflove2020
	@The Rules of a Big Boss